Courageous Gilbert
the Groundhog

by Regina E. McCarthy

Illustrated by Sue Dettman

Courageous Gilbert the Groundhog

Published by
Blue Stone Healing Books
545 Tollgate Road, Suite B ■ Elgin, Illinois 60123
www.courageousgilbert.com

ISBN: 978-0-9862304-1-7

Publisher's Cataloging-In-Publication Data
(Prepared by The Donohue Group, Inc.)

McCarthy, Regina E.
    Courageous Gilbert the groundhog / by Regina E. McCarthy ; illustrated by Sue Dettman.

        pages : illustrations ; cm

    Summary: Courageous Gilbert the Groundhog has stage fright, no friends, and a bully out to get him. But, when he learns how to relax his body, how to feel his emotions, and when to express them, he confidently presents at an after-school club, makes a new friend, and stands up to the bully.
    Interest age level: Juvenile.
    ISBN: 978-0-9862304-1-7

    1. Woodchuck—Juvenile fiction. 2. Emotions in children—Juvenile fiction. 3. Courage in children—Juvenile fiction. 4. Bullying—Juvenile fiction. 5. Woodchuck—Fiction. 6. Emotions—Fiction. 7. Courage—Fiction. 8. Bullying—Fiction. I. Dettman, Sue. II. Title.

PZ7.1.M33 Co 2015
[E]   2015901729

Illustrations by Sue Dettman

Editor: Gail M. Kearns, www.topressandbeyond.com
Art Director: Penelope Paine, www.topressandbeyond.com
Typography: Cirrus Book Design
Production coordinated by To Press & Beyond

Printed in the
United States of America

To my amazing family,
George, Colin, Dylan,
and Tara.

Gilbert was a great collector. He collected toy cars, action figures, and lots of rocks.

He also loved listening to his favorite music on his headphones while he sang along as loud as he could.

But there were some things Gilbert did not enjoy.

He was shy and didn't like standing up in front of the class. He didn't like finding someone to sit with at lunch, and he didn't like being made fun of when he sang. Doing those things made his stomach jump and his knees shake and his heart pound.

Today was like the other days at school. Peter Opossum teased him about his singing, and no one made a space for him at the lunch table.

6

Gilbert was very upset. He dumped his lunch tray and raced as fast as he could across the playground where he climbed up an old oak tree.

"I hate school," Gilbert muttered to himself as he clawed his way up the tree.

"Ouch," a soft voice called out. "Be careful of my bark."

Gilbert was startled. "Whoa, who said that?" he asked.

"I did," the Old Oak Tree answered. "I do not like my bark being pulled and clawed."

"Sorry!" Gilbert said. "I was upset. Are you for real?"

"Well, of course I am. I'm as real as you are." The Old Oak Tree gently rustled its branches. "Now, tell me why you are so upset."

7

"I hate talking in front of the class," Gilbert sighed. "And Peter Opossum makes fun of me when I sing. Nobody wants to be my friend."

"Hmmm," the tree said kindly. "Maybe I can help. We can't change Peter Opossum, but I can teach you a way to feel better, all the way from your head to your toes. Would you like that? Why don't you come on down and sit in my shade?"

Gilbert wondered how the Old Oak Tree could know about feeling better, especially because the tree didn't have a head or any toes at all. But it sounded very good to him, and he nodded so hard that he almost fell off the branch.

Gilbert climbed down and sat at the base of the tree. "First, I want you to close your eyes," the Old Oak Tree instructed.

Gilbert closed his eyes tight.

"Now, take a deep
breath in, all the
way to your belly.
In through your
nose...

10

and out through your mouth."

As Gilbert began to breathe in and out, the tree whispered in Gilbert's ear.

Breathe - in - for - four.

Hold - this - heaven - till - count - of - seven.

Exhale - for - eight - and - you - will - feel - great!

Breathe - in - for - four.

Hold - this - heaven - till - count - of - seven.

Exhale - for- eight - and - you - will - feel - great!

Breathe - in - for - four.

Hold - this - heaven - till - count - of - seven.

Exhale -for- eight - and - you - will - feel - great!

After a few deep breaths, Gilbert's head felt much better, and his stomach stopped rolling around, and best of all his heart stopped thumping. His whole body felt happy.

"Wow!" Gilbert said, smiling. "That IS much better. Old Oak Tree, how does it work?"

"It is called deep breathing," the Old Oak Tree said. "And it helps every part of your body feel safe. So, next time Peter Opossum teases you or you have to stand up in front of the class, remember the rhyme and do some deep breathing."

Gilbert heard the bell ring.

"I have to go now," he told the Old Oak Tree. "Can I come and see you again?"

"Of course," the tree said. "I will always be here."

Gilbert hummed his favorite song all the way back to class.

The next day, it was Gilbert's turn to share his book report in class.
When he walked to the front of the room, his hands began to shake.
When he spoke, his voice quivered.
His cheeks burned red.
The hair on his tail stood on end.
And he forgot what he was going to say.

His classmates laughed, especially Peter Opossum.

I can't do this. I can't do this! the voice in Gilbert's head kept saying.

Gilbert wanted to feel the way he did when the Old Oak Tree had helped him.

He imagined he could hear the tree whispering in his ear.

17

Breathe - in - for - four.

Hold - this - heaven - till - count - of - seven.

Exhale - for - eight - and - you - will - feel - great!

Breathe - in - for - four.

Hold - this - heaven - till - count - of - seven.

Exhale - for- eight - and - you - will - feel - great!

Breathe - in - for - four.

Hold - this - heaven - till - count - of - seven.

Exhale - for- eight - and - you - will - feel - great!

By lunchtime, Gilbert was feeling a little better, and he ran to the Old Oak Tree.

"Hey," he panted, "I did what you said, but it didn't help when I was in front of the class."

The Old Oak Tree smiled.
"Tell me how your body
feels when you are in front
of the class."

"Well, my hands get really
sweaty, my stomach is full
of butterflies, and I forget
what to say!"

The Old Oak Tree listened
carefully. "And when no one
makes room for you at the
lunch table, is it the same?"

Gilbert thought for a
minute. "That's when my
heart feels very sad and sort
of heavy."

"And when Peter Opossum makes fun of your singing?" the tree asked.

Gilbert's lips tightened. "I feel stuck inside, and I can hardly breathe! I just want to run away."

"Ahhh, Gilbert," the Old Oak Tree sighed. "You are feeling your emotions. I feel mine too. They can be in your heart, in your stomach, or anywhere in your body."

The bell rang, and Gilbert said good-bye to the Old Oak Tree.
"Don't forget to practice your breathing." The Old Oak Tree waved
a branch, and Gilbert waved back.

Gilbert did not understand all the Old Oak Tree had taught him,
but he was glad he had someone to talk with about it.

When Gilbert returned the next day, the tree asked, "How was school today?"

"Terrible," Gilbert answered quickly. "It doesn't work!"

"What doesn't work?" the Old Oak Tree asked, bending over to hear more clearly.

Gilbert was shaking. "The breathing. I *still* get so upset when I hear the kids laughing at me."

"Do you know why?" the tree asked.

"No," Gilbert answered.

"Because as well as *feeling* your emotions, you also have to *express* them."

"Express my emotions? What does that mean?" Gilbert asked.

"It means getting your feelings out so you can feel better. You have to do this AND breathe. If you practice, it will get easier. But you have to practice.

"The next time you feel scared, go outside and scream into your hands. If you feel sad, you can sigh or cry. Then, when someone makes fun of you, tell them that's not okay and to please stop."

Gilbert thought for a while. "I'll try, but it's really, *really* hard."

"I know," the tree said. "It takes courage to feel and share your emotions. You need to let them out, just like when you sing. Don't hide them inside."

That night, Gilbert practiced his **mad** feelings by stomping his feet on the floor, roaring into his hands, and yelling into his pillow.

Then Gilbert practiced his **sad** feelings. He sighed big sighs, and he cried a whole bucket of tears.

The next day, he practiced his courage and marched around the Old Oak Tree, saying, "Peter Opossum, it's not okay to talk to me like that. I feel hurt when you laugh at me. Don't treat me that way."

Every day he practiced, and every day he found a little more courage. Slowly, slowly, slowly, over time, Gilbert began to change. He was less shy and not so scared of Peter Opossum.

26

Pretty soon, Gilbert shared his rock collection at the after-school Rock Club, and his stomach only had two little butterflies in it.

His classmate Aileen heard him humming her favorite tune. "Gilbert, I love that song," she said. So they decided to listen to music together after school.

But best of all, when Peter Opossum called out, "Hey Gilbert, let's hear your crummy voice," Gilbert took a deep breath, and although his knees were knocking, he reached inside and found his courage. "Peter Opossum, cut that out," he said firmly. "Stop bugging me. I've had enough."

Peter was so surprised that when he opened his mouth to answer back, nothing came out!

Gilbert felt a rush of pride. *I did it! I really did it! I stood up to Peter Opossum!*

Gilbert had a big smile on his face, and his legs wanted to dance. His whole body felt happy.

"Hey, Old Oak Tree," Gilbert called out. "I did it! I stood up to Peter Opossum."

"I knew you could!" the tree said. "You found your courage, and I'm so proud of you."

From then on, Gilbert found it easier and easier to find his courage. He breathed deeply every day, felt his emotions, and expressed them. He knew this was the only way to take care of himself. It felt awesome!

And, whenever he listened to his music, Gilbert sang as loud as he could.

A Message for Parents, Teachers, and Other Caring Adults

Courageous Gilbert the Groundhog is a delightful book rich in symbolism written for children and adults. Read it and practice the techniques below with your children, students, clients, and friends.

When working with children, and adults, it helps to first calm the body with deep breathing. If the body is in a state of panic or shock, it will go into the fight, flight, or freeze mode, making healthy responses more difficult. Deep breathing calms the entire nervous system, oxygenates the brain, and creates a safe feeling in the body. Deep breathing can be done at the beginning of the day, at lunch, and before going to bed. Over time, the benefits multiply as the body relaxes and feels less anxious.

We need to teach about emotions. Identifying where emotions are held in the body and how to express them is vital. Emotions tell us who we are, what we like and do not like. Fear indicates we need to get safe, anger helps us set boundaries, and sadness lets us know there is something we need to release. If we are numb to our emotions, we feel victimized and unable to stand up for ourselves. Unexpressed emotions can lead to dis-ease. Identifying and releasing our emotions empowers us to be our authentic selves, or who we are meant to be.

We are what we practice. This healing process takes time, and practicing can be done as a class, family, or in a group. Practice involves yelling into your hands, stomping your feet on the ground, and saying "It is not okay to talk to me like that. You need to stop." And then practice walking away. Too often we are stuck and not aware that we have the choice to leave. A final practice is shaking it off. Literally.

The breathing technique in this book is called "The 4, 7, 8, Breathing for Relaxation." I learned it from Dr. Andrew Weil's book *8 Weeks to Optimum Health* and have been teaching it to my children and their classmates since 2004.

Regina E. McCarthy

Regina E. McCarthy, LCSW, is a Holistic Psychotherapist with a private practice in Elgin, IL. She received her undergraduate degree from Boston College, Boston, MA, and her master's in social work from Loyola University, Chicago, IL. She is a member of the National Association of Social Workers and the Wellness Institute, Issaquah, WA. She is an Advanced Heart-Centered Hypnotherapist®, an Integral Breathwork therapist, a Trim-Life® provider, and a Reiki Master. She lives with her husband and has three adult children and a cat named Bob. *Courageous Gilbert the Groundhog* is her first book.

Sue Dettman lives with her husband, Tom, in Elgin, IL. Sue has been illustrating children's curriculum and story books for over forty years. She also writes children's curriculum and does watercolor and graphic design.